STUFF
EVERY BRIDE
SHOULD KNOW

Stuff Every

Bride

Should Know

By Michelle Park Lazette

QUIRK BOOKS

PHILADELPHIA

Copyright © 2015 by Quirk Productions, Inc.

All rights reserved. No part of this book may be reproduced
in any form without written permission from the publisher.

Library of Congress Cataloging in Publication Number: 2014956804

ISBN: 978-1-59474-833-2

Printed in China
Typeset in Adobe Garamond Pro, Montserrat, and Gill Sans

Cover design by Alisa Wismer
Production management by John J. McGurk

Quirk Books
215 Church Street
Philadelphia, PA 19106
quirkbooks.com

10   9   8   7   6   5   4

To the loves of my life:
Steven, Steph, and Mom. Without you,
the bride I was and the woman I am
wouldn't be possible.

DETAIL STUFF

WEDDING (AND BEYOND) STUFF

Introduction

What a rush. You're getting married. You'll be the bride!

Get ready: Everyone will have an opinion (with the possible exception, infuriatingly, of your partner). Your vendors will offer their best practices. (Take them.) Parents will voice their expectations. (Navigate them.) Google Images will drown you in ideas. (Be discerning.)

You hold in your hands the book I wish I'd had when a wedding was mine to plan—one that covers the must-ask questions, the general timeline by which things should fall into place, and the warnings that can help prevent regrets. But just because it offers tips for hiring a florist and a DJ doesn't mean you have to enlist either. Focus on the stuff that resonates with you, and skip the stuff that doesn't. Your wedding day should be remembered more for how it felt than for what you spent.

After all, the big picture is this: You're one of the lucky ones. Someone loves you so much they want to spend the rest of this finite, fleeting life with you, and you feel the same way. Not everyone strikes it so rich.

So read this Stuff, consume only as many Pinterest wedding boards as you can stand, and trust in yourself, your vendors, and, most of all, your soon-to-be spouse. You've got a long life together full of adventure and milestones, and this is just the beginning.

First

Stuff

First

.

What to Do Now That You're Engaged

The question has been asked and answered, and now it's time to celebrate. Here's some advice for your first days as a fiancée.

- Share the news. Tell the people closest to you first, in person if possible. If you don't want news of your engagement to leak before you announce it, ask people to keep a lid on it, especially on social media.

- Paint your fingernails. Speaking of sharing the news in person, eyes are about to gravitate to your hands. If manicures are your thing, now's as good a time as ever to get one.

- Get your story straight. People will ask how you got engaged—and maybe even how you met—so decide what you do (and don't) want to say.

- Enjoy yourself. Give yourself some time to enjoy your engagement before diving into wedding planning. You will have plenty of time to make decisions after you've come down from the high. You may even want to plan an engagement party or schedule an engagement photo session.

- **Don't promise invitations yet.** If someone asks if they'll see an invite, you can always reply that you hope so but you're not sure how the details (like your budget) will unfold. You don't want to have to disinvite them later—or feel obligated to invite them because you spoke too soon.

- **Be vague about your plans.** Resist the urge to advertise the accoutrements your day will have, even if you've had your heart set on them since you were twelve. You never know what plans will change.

Six Questions to Ask Your Intended

Planning a giant party is fun, but be sure to take some time now to plan the marriage it's celebrating. Consider seeking premarital counseling, which can provide you with tools for communicating well throughout your lifetime together. Here are just a few of the questions you should discuss before saying "I do." Keep in mind: the answers may change over the years.

1. **Do you want kids?** Six months after the wedding is not the time to discover that your spouse doesn't want a single child.

2. **What are your religious beliefs?** And will you raise those potential children to follow them?

3. **What are your career plans?** Are you willing to move away from where you live to follow them— or to follow your spouse's? Do either of you want to stay at home with your children?

4. **What do your finances look like?** You should know about one another's credit histories, preferences for saving and spending, and debts.

5. **How do you show love?** Everyone is different, and there are many different ways to express love. Some of us do the dishes or perform other caretaking roles. Others feed off of physical affection. Recognize how your spouse-to-be demonstrates and receives love.

6. **How do you fight?** How do you act when you're upset? Are you confrontational? Do you need your space at first? Take this opportunity to commit to healthy fighting. Know and respect each other's boundaries. Even in times of friction, be giving. Marriage works when you commit to making it work. That commitment is required well beyond the honeymoon and is especially important in times of strife.

How to Insure Your Ring . . . and Your Wedding

It may not be the most romantic item on your to-do list, but insuring your engagement ring is important, so do it as soon as you can. Here are some tips from insurance broker Pete Pappadakes.

- Don't assume that your renter's or homeowner's insurance will cover your jewelry. In fact, such policies tend to offer very limited coverage for anything that is highly valuable and highly portable. You will probably need to add a separate, additional policy.

- Get your ring appraised, and provide your insurance company with the appraisal, which includes details about the stone's cut, color, clarity, and carat weight that can be replicated in the event of loss.

- The rule of thumb for the cost of coverage is $10 per $1,000 of appraised worth, annually. That is, if your ring is appraised at $7,000, expect to pay roughly $70 a year to insure it.

- All of this applies to wedding bands, too.

You can also insure the wedding itself. Wedding insurance provides coverage in the event of natural catastrophes, something going wrong with your venue, and more. It can also provide liability coverage to protect you against claims should a guest be injured or injure someone on the way home. More from Pete:

- You may think you don't need wedding insurance, but give it special consideration if there's a higher chance of something going wrong—for example, if your wedding will be outdoors or if you will have a lot of family traveling a considerable distance to attend.

- Wedding insurance comes with restrictions if you purchase it close to the event date, so buy early if there's cause for concern.

- The premiums for wedding insurance tend to be a function of how large your wedding and its costs are. Don't skimp, because you will likely spend more than you think you will on the wedding.

- Be sure to ask the agent about the policy's exclusions (i.e., the reasons why it wouldn't cover a loss).

- Wedding insurance, unlike jewelry insurance, is sold as a standalone policy instead of an add-on to your existing insurance. But it can't hurt to ask if you can score a discount by getting both at the same time.

And while we're talking about insurance: if you and your partner are moving into a rental apartment together, now is the time to get renter's insurance. Your landlord's policy usually will *not* cover your belongings—including your lovely wedding gifts—in the event of a loss (fire, smoke damage, flooding, etc.).

Picturing Your Wedding

Was planning a wedding easier or harder before social media made us aware of everyone else's supremely creative, must-steal ideas? All that inspiration can get overwhelming. Stay calm, and start here:

1. **Decide on your style.** Before you start scanning Instagram and Pinterest, reflect on yourselves as a couple. What kind of wedding would cause people to depart remarking, "That was so *them*"?

2. **Decide on your wedding's style.** Is it rustic and laid-back? Glitzy and formal? Modern and somewhere in between?

3. ***Now* head to Pinterest.** Once you've narrowed your vision at least a little, let the inspiration foraging begin. Wedding blogs, social media, magazines, and books offer a ton of resources. Compile pictures of things you adore and are interested in trying. Don't forget that you don't have to do everything!

4. **Step outside the box.** Your day will feel more authentic if you choose to personalize it, even if just in the details. Only you can decide how to

best achieve that. Maybe it's an extensive craft beer selection if you're beer enthusiasts, or wedding karaoke if you met at a karaoke bar.

5. **Stick with your style.** Once you've chosen your wedding's style, match the other elements of your day to it. Otherwise you may end up with unintentional incongruity—for example, having a pig roast at a supremely formal wedding could feel a little odd.

Choosing Your Guests

Before you invite 350 people to your wedding, consider this: you're expected to greet all your guests at the reception. Catching up, even briefly, with so many people will consume a hefty chunk of time. There are only so many hours in your wedding night. Here are some tips for writing the guest list.

- **Write an A list and a B list.** Put the people you truly want to invite—not just because they invited you to their weddings or because they're your distant cousins—on the A list, and send their invitations early. When the RSVPs start arriving and you learn that some A-listers won't make it, mail invitations to a corresponding number of B-listers. (Plan this far enough in advance that B-listers have time to reply before the RSVP date.)

- **Ask your families.** Consider asking your closest family members whom they'd like to see invited. Weddings are more fun when you know other people, and your nearest and dearest should enjoy themselves. If Mom and Dad ask to invite so many people that it reduces how many friends you can invite, ask them to cover the costs of some of their guests (if they aren't already).

- **Include your guests' guests.** Be thoughtful about offering your guests a date. Allowing someone who doesn't know many of your other friends to bring a plus-one guarantees that she will feel at ease, but offering everyone a date can quickly inflate your invitation list. Find a balance that works for you.

- **Deal with the uninvited.** In today's social-media-laden world, people will know when you're getting married—and when they've not been invited. If they ask why, deflect blame to the venue's capacity or to your own budgetary restraints, or simply explain that you're planning a more intimate gathering. They'll get over it.

How to Set a Budget

You could easily spend tens of thousands of dollars on a wedding, but that doesn't mean you *must*. Be resourceful and prioritize. No matter your budget, you can have at least some of the fabulous ideas that you dream up.

- **Set your limits.** Calculate how much you can afford to spend on your wedding. If your parents are planning to contribute financially, now is the time to talk about it, even if you feel awkward bringing it up. Explain that you're trying to set and stick to a budget, and you wonder what, if anything, they'd like to contribute. If the answer is nothing, be gracious and don't feel discouraged. The important thing is that you know a firm number before you start planning.

- **Start saving.** Need to save more money than you ever have before? Deposit part of each paycheck into a savings account at an institution that's not your mainstay. What you can't see, you won't spend. Use the account to pay for all of your wedding-related expenses. After the wedding, you can close it . . . or change its purpose to your next big goal!

- **Make a wish list.** Prioritize which details are most important to you. (If you're high-end-food lovers, settling for delivery pizza may not appeal to you.) You don't want to have written checks for ancillary details only to realize that the locally sourced, upscale menu items you wanted are unaffordable with the dollars that remain.

- **Do some research.** Blindly setting a budget for something you've never purchased doesn't make sense. So before you assign numbers to what you'll spend on linens and uplighting, research them. Call three vendors in each category and ask the going rate for their services and what they'll include.

- **Add it up.** Estimate how much you expect to spend on each item of your wish list, and know the subtotal. Then build in some extra space for unexpected expenses. Is the total less than the limit you set? Lucky you! Is it more? Try cutting some lower-priority line items, reducing the guest list, or swapping in some alternatives until the amount you plan to spend is less than the amount you can afford.

- **Stick to the plan.** Refer to your budget as you start hiring vendors, buying supplies, and signing contracts. You can adjust it, but remember to keep it balanced. If you're going to spend more on the photographer, spend less on the flowers to allow for it.

- **Be careful of too-good deals.** The higher the demand for someone's photography, wedding planning, or pie pops, the more they can charge. It's simple supply and demand, and that's fair—after all, they're vendors, not nonprofits. So before you hire a bottom-dollar vendor, figure out why their prices are so low. They may have less experience, for example, or they may source cheaper supplies.

- **Offer to barter.** Don't feel ashamed asking vendors: How can we cut costs while still achieving our goals? Is there something you need (writing, photography, marketing help, an extra pair of hands for wedding setups, etc.) for which you'd consider a trade or discount?

- **Put away the credit card.** Don't go into debt for your wedding, especially if you're only racking it up because the day has become a production that you presume everyone expects. You can spend an entire year's salary and still disappoint someone. As you set sail for your honeymoon, the day should be a memory, and so should its costs.

How to Set the Date

Finally—everyone's favorite well-meant question will have an answer! For the most part, it's as easy as picking a date that works for you. But keep these potential pitfalls and practicalities in mind.

- **Weather.** What might be too hot or too cold for a wedding in your area? Think about your guests' comfort. Chances are slim that anyone wants to spend your outdoor ceremony sweating or shivering, and you don't want the weather to distract from your day (which inclement conditions would).

- **Holidays.** Think hard before you force your guests to celebrate you on a day that they'd usually spend with family. Another argument for not marrying on a holiday weekend: Hotel and flight costs tend to increase, and weddings are already expensive enough for all involved. Those caveats aside, who doesn't love a party on New Year's Eve? And extended holiday weekends are convenient if you want to marry on a Sunday but hope that your guests can stay late to celebrate.

- **Your favorite season.** If you look forward to autumn's crunchy leaves or spring's cherry blossoms every year, marry when they'll be present to frame your day.

- **Your favorite vendor.** If you have a wedding vendor you can't marry without, check availability before choosing a specific date.

- **You can't please everyone.** We all receive regrets. There's always someone who can't make it, so don't try to schedule around absolutely everyone.

- **Off-season dates.** Choosing a less-crowded date can afford you discounts but also can require sacrifice. Many flowers will be unavailable or more costly for a winter wedding, for example. And snowfall on your big day may mean some guests can't make the trip. Your vendors can tell you when their off-season is and if booking then will save you money.

- **Fridays and Sundays.** Supply and demand: days of the week that are less popular than Saturday can save you money.

- **Timing.** Planning a wedding quickly can be hectic—and expensive. It also might force you to forgo details you simply don't have time for (a custom wedding gown, for example) and vendors that are already booked.

- Meaning. Your favorite number, a special family date, or a dating anniversary can make for meaningful choices.

Choosing Your Reception Venue

Your venue is where you'll make your grandest entrance. Dance your first married dance. Watch everything you've planned fall into place. (Or fall apart—it happens to the best of us.) Here are some pointers for choosing the perfect place.

Decide how many people to invite *first*. Some venues can easily accommodate a 200-person wedding, but 200 people will cram like sardines inside others. Ask about maximum capacity.

Pick a place that reflects your theme. A barn wedding inside a barn feels more authentic than a barn wedding inside a hotel ballroom. Finding a place that exudes your "feel" naturally is easier and less expensive than forcing it. Think oceanfront for nautical, an era-appropriate mansion for vintage, or a Christmas tree farm for winter wonderland.

Ask a vendor you trust for advice. Your vendors have seen a lot of weddings!

Consider your local park and pavilion. Rental often costs a nominal fee or nothing, but make sure to reserve it with the local parks and recreation department.

Be wary of location-only venues. Don't get bewitched by an unbelievably affordable venue that offers only its space. Some venues handle almost everything (from bartending to linens), and others don't handle a thing. Lining up vendors and decorating yourself are perfectly doable projects, but they're also much more time-consuming. Do you have it in you to quarterback as much as you will need to? We can't all be Peyton Manning.

Rural or urban? Rural locations tend to cost less than downtown city locales. They may also be farther away from your guests' accommodations, so strike the right balance.

Will you need climate control? Be sure to ask when the air conditioning or heat will be turned on—only an hour beforehand may not always do the trick.

Think you've just seen The Place? View it by day and at night. If you'll have only an hour of daylight during your reception, the gorgeous waterfront view won't be visible for very long. And don't forget, a dark room during the day typically is even darker at night.

Bring the shoes you plan to wear for a test. If you'll be outside, note if your heels sink into the grass or dirt. (You can invest in heel protectors, but you want to be able to walk comfortably.)

Pick a place where you can be yourself. Don't choose something because it's "wedding appropriate" if it makes you feel like a bull in a china shop. Your guests will be more comfortable if you are.

Choosing Your Ceremony Venue

For some, this decision begins and ends in the pews they sat in every Sunday growing up. For others, a sandy beach or some other locale calls. And others simply want a place where the ceremony and reception can take place within feet of each other.

Questions to Ask Yourself

☐ How far away will the reception be?

☐ How will people get to the ceremony, and then to the reception? If they must drive, where will they park?

☐ Where will you make your entrance?

☐ Look at the altar/gazebo space. Is there enough room for the bridal party you've selected to move around?

☐ Is there enough space for the bridal party to get ready? Does the space have the lighting and amenities you want?

☐ Does the aisle look wide enough for your dress and the person or people who will escort you? What about people with strollers, walkers, or wheelchairs?

☐ Is this venue accessible to all your guests? How far will they need to walk, and how many stairs will they need to climb?

☐ How do the acoustics sound?

☐ If the ceremony will be outside, what's plan B if the weather disobeys? When would the call need to be made? Who would handle the logistics?

Questions to Ask the Venue

☐ What's maximum capacity? Is there enough room for my guests? Is there too much room? (You don't want it to look empty!)

☐ Does this space have climate control, and how far in advance will you turn on the heat or air-conditioning?

☐ What sound equipment is available to accommodate my ceremony? Ask about speakers, piano and other instruments, microphones, etc.

☐ What types of decorations and music are allowed?

☐ Is there a dress code?

☐ Is there a church/site coordinator?

☐ Can my photographer and videographer move freely throughout the space? Can they use flash photography?

☐ Is there a nursery area for infants and children?

☐ Will I be able to rehearse here the day or night before? (If you can't because there will be another wedding in the space, rehearse somewhere else, facing the same direction as you will in the big moment.)

Big
Picture
Stuff

How to Pick Your Photographer and Love Your Photos

Photography is one of the most lasting investments in your wedding day that you can make. The food will be eaten. The music will bump and then unplug. But the photos can capture some of the feeling for posterity.

Decide what style of photographs you want. Artistic? Documentary? Browse the photographer's portfolio, and ask to see images other than those on the website, which will always be their best work. Do the images tell each couple's story, or are they the same for everyone? Avoid hiring a photographer who has little experience, a less-than-stunning portfolio, or few, if any, positive reviews.

The following questions can serve as a guide in your quest for the best keepsake images.

What to Ask the Photographer

- How many weddings have you shot?
- Do you bring backup equipment?
- Do you provide a disk of images and the rights for their use? You'll need a release in order to print images, order canvases, etc.

- Who will photograph our wedding? Be sure the photographer whose portfolio you like will be the person who shoots your wedding. Does your photographer have an assistant who shoots when he or she can't be in two places at once?

- How many hours are included in the package? If there are early-bird or late-night shots on your must-shoot list, you'll want to know if you'll incur overtime fees.

- When will we receive our photos?

Shoot List

Making a list ahead of time will help ensure that your photographer doesn't miss any special moments. Here are some must-haves to include.

☐ Action shots of the ceremony.

☐ Family and wedding party portraits.

☐ The scenery.

☐ Getting-ready shots.

☐ Unique shots. Images that other brides might not prioritize, like the newlyweds sitting on a swing set or holding a "thank you" sign (to be used on thank-you cards, of course!).

☐ **Details.** You probably spent months on them, so get a shot of the centerpiece jars.

☐ **First look.** Many brides are stealing away for a private "reveal" with their betrothed before the ceremony, a moment that's called the "first look."

Hiring a Videographer

Photographs only go so far. Video of your big day lets you hear the toasts and your vows all over again. The day itself will be a blur, but with videography you can get some of it back fovever.

As with photography, it's helpful to give your videographer a must-shoot list. Ask prospective videographers the same questions you ask photographers, and add these too.

- May I watch a few sample videos you've produced for past clients?

- What can you tell me about your equipment? How do you ensure clear audio?

- What will the end product include?

How to Pick a Planner

Wedding planners' services run the gamut; they can plan weddings from the get-go or offer month-of and day-of coordination. Ask your prospective planners:

- How many weddings have you planned, and over what span of time? Why do you do this?

- Who are three vendors you'd recommend we consider? (You want someone plugged into the local wedding community.)

- Can you find items we may borrow?

- How would you handle [*insert scenario that gives you the obligatory wedding nightmare*]?

- What's your rate, and what specifically are we paying you to do?

Feeding Your Guests

Take a bite out of menu planning one step at a time, and you'll serve up food that's sure to be memorable for all the right reasons.

Each of the various service styles has pros and cons, so consider these points as you picture the reception of your dreams.

- **Buffet** tends to be cheaper but feels less upscale and involves self-service and lines (though these are easily limited by staggering the timing that each table queues up).

- **Family-style**, in which platters of food are placed at and passed around each table, is another less expensive choice that's convenient for guests, but customization of the meal is limited. (Because, really, how many different dishes do you want crowding each table?)

- **Stations**, where staffers make and/or serve varied cuisine for guests (for example, pasta and carving stations), offer variety but cost more because you need more cooks on-site.

- **Plated** dinners are often regarded as the most tra-ditional and classiest service style, but the servers will cost you more, and guests tend to have less choice of cuisine.

So where's a bride to start?

Find a Caterer

- **Get recommendations.** Ask other couples and the vendors you trust. Read online reviews of caterers in your wedding locale.

- **Ask for references,** and check them. Read health department records in the county where the caterer operates. These reveal whether the company has frequent violations, ranging from food temperatures to hand-washing practices.

- **Understand the caterer's prices.** Many will charge you for the food, drink service, manpower required, china and flatware, and cake cutting. You want to know what your money is buying and, perhaps more important, what it's not.

- **Taste!** Usually a taste test is yours for the taking. So take it! Revel in one of the funner parts of wedding planning. And be vocal about what you like and don't like. The taste of your food is paramount. Appearance is important, too.

- **Listen.** What's arguably most vital once you've chosen a caterer is listening. Piping hot pasta presented the way each guests orders it sounds tasty, but doing dinner this way can mean long waits for the last people served. Listen when the caterer warns you. Caterers will also know which foods hold up well in a buffet and which will become soggy or dry out. Ask them to innovate all you like, but don't expect them to perform miracles.

Draw Up Your Menu

It helps to narrow down what to serve. These tips will ensure a successful short list.

- **Pick food to fit your venue, theme, or wedding date.** Tying the knot in a coastal city? Fresh fish makes sense. Planning a November wedding? How about turkey and thyme-and-sage-spiced stuffing drowning in gravy?

- **Think of your guests.** Choose food that's a reflection of you two, but remember: you want your guests to enjoy themselves. Think twice before serving molten-hot curry or leaving vegans and vegetarians to graze upon green beans and almonds alone. (Odds are, your caterer will be happy to serve vegetarian options. Be sure to ask your guests for their preferences.)

- **Plan beyond six o'clock.** There's no rule that prohibits you from marrying in the morning and serving a brunch or lunch at the reception. And if there's a wait between your ceremony and dinner, bear in mind that your guests might want to nibble on something in between. Finally, if you expect your crowd to exhibit staying power, consider a late-night snack via your caterer, a pizza deliveryman, or a food truck.

Day-Of Advice: Be Sure to Eat!

You might not feel hungry. Being watched and celebrated by so many people can be surreal. The moments fly by. Absorb the day, but make time to eat. You need your energy, and drinking on an empty stomach is not a recipe for remembering your big night.

Worried it'll be hard to find the time to eat? Ask your wedding planner or DJ to ensure you find it. They'll know how.

Stocking the Bar

Whether your venue is serving up the gin and juice or you are, you have plenty of options for personalizing the bar and controlling costs (if you want to).

Think twice before opting for a cash bar. Asking your guests to pay to drink is akin to asking them to pay for the dinners you've selected for them. If the budget's tight, limit your bar to beer and wine, or offer beer and wine plus a few mixed drinks. Do you and your spouse-to-be share an affinity for a certain cocktail? Serve it as the signature drink.

If your venue allows you to BYOB, stocking the bar is a chance to share your favorite choices with your guests. When you buy the alcohol, try to negotiate to buy on commission, which means the distributor will take back unopened cases.

If stocking the bar yourself, follow these tips.

- Display a list of drinks. Doing so saves your bartender from having to repeat the list each time.

- Speaking of bartenders, hire one. An unsupervised bar can get messy—in more ways than one. Another huge benefit: seasoned bartenders can accurately estimate how much alcohol you will need for a party your size. Some even bring their own garnishes and mixers.

- Don't forget ice and glasses. Some caterers will provide stemware. You can also buy bulk boxes of disposable glasses online, or your distributor might be able to secure them for you.

Don't want to serve alcohol at all? Unless you're inviting people who live a teetotaler life, a dry evening wedding might disappoint guests. Instead, consider holding your event at an earlier time of day. People are less likely to expect a buzz in the morning or early afternoon.

Dreaming Up Dessert

Few parts of wedding planning taste as good as dessert does. Welcome to your obligatory sugar high.

You can let them eat cake, or not. Nowadays, many couples are opting not to bow to the convention of a traditional three-tier, fondant-laden wedding cake. There are cupcake towers. Cookie rooms. Candy tables. Pie pops.

Before deciding what your final course will be, consider these options.

- **Coordinate dessert with your theme.** Circus wedding? Step right up for funnel cakes and cotton candy. Summer nuptials? Refresh with root beer floats. Or roast some s'mores at a fall wedding.

- **Make your favorite.** Some people don't fawn over cake. Serve a dessert your spouse-to-be practically begs you to make at home or one that reminds you of a special time or person.

- **Dish up variety.** Choose multiple flavors of cupcakes (opt for bite-sized, so guests don't fill up on the first flavor they try). Or go for waffles, cheesecake, *and* cream puffs.

- **Serve something allergy-friendly.** Many bakers can whip up gluten-free, kosher, and vegan options. Given the vast array of desserts with nuts, you may want to label those that have them, in case you have guests who need to know.

Here are some questions to ask potential treats vendors:

- **May I have references?** Make sure to see a portfolio of work the vendors did themselves, and schedule a tasting.

- **What cake and filling flavors are available?** Expect to pay more for nontraditional fillings.

- **What do you charge for delivery?**

- **How do you keep sweets at the right temperature?** Cake frosting can melt in the heat of summer, but more important, you want a baker who plans ahead so that refrigerated dessert items have time to come to room temperature before being served.

- **Is the top tier of the cake included?** This is the part traditionally saved for your one-year anniversary.

Cutting the Cake (Costs)

Many venues and caterers charge a cake-cutting fee. Couple that fee with the price your baker charges per slice, and your slices easily end up costing several dollars each.

Trying to trim the cost? Order fewer slices than guests, since it's unlikely everyone will eat cake. Or order an adorned, smaller cake for the cake-cutting tradition, but serve sheet cake (kept out of sight) to guests. They'll never know.

How to Select Your Soundtrack

Music permeates most parts of your wedding day. And as with other parts of a wedding, the music is most memorable when it fits the two of you. That's not to say you should play only the '90s hits or the Metallica tunes you sing in the shower. The dance floor might prove emptier than you'd hoped if your soundtrack isn't accessible to the majority of your guests. Play a good mix.

Put thought into your ceremony music, too. Avoid strange song choices for moments when all eyes are on you.

Here are some questions to ask yourself:

- Do you have songs that are must-plays? Are those must-plays music you can dance to? If they aren't, ask to hear them during dinner.

- Will you let guests make song requests? This is where a do-not-play list comes in handy.

- Are you philosophically opposed to line dances? There's every chance your guests will request them.

- **Do you want to include your guests in traditional dances?** Extending moments like the father-daughter dance, for example, would mean inviting your guests to dance with their dads, too. It could pack the dance floor early.

Finding a DJ

Don't presume that all a DJ does is play music and that a streaming music service is a foolproof stand-in. A reputable, professional DJ manages the timeline and the crowd—announcing your grand entrance, playing the music they observe your crowd really gets into, and ensuring that dinner music is not too loud or grating for conversation. Most DJs also offer uplighting, or lighting concentrated in an upward direction, often placed along walls and behind the head table. It elevates the look of a room.

Be sure to find a DJ with master-of-ceremonies skills, someone who will announce special moments only after ensuring you're ready for them, someone who will take the time to learn how to pronounce names correctly, someone who has personality . . . but not one that's self-serving.

Here are some questions to ask a prospective DJ.

- **How do you personalize wedding receptions?** Pick up on it when a DJ tells you how he or she usually does things. Do you want the same party he hosted last week for someone else?

- **If we request a song before our event that you don't presently have in your library, will you obtain it?**

- **How will you plan to play our particular venue?** You want someone who will do their homework to make sure they bring what they need and set up appropriately.

- **How do you hide your equipment?** Draping can ensure your venue doesn't look like an electronics store.

- **What will you wear?**

- **How many hours are included in this package?** Know what constitutes overtime.

- **What's your contingency plan in the event of illness or equipment failure?**

- **May we see some references and clips of your past work?** Although some may offer, don't expect all DJs to invite you to see them play a wedding. Would you want your DJ welcoming strangers to your wedding reception? .

Finding a Band

If you prefer live music, go for it. Be sure to ask about a musician's or band's style and specialty and the music clips you've heard. Are they live, untouched ones, or technically enhanced? Can a member of the band act as master of ceremonies? Be sure to ask the band all the bulleted questions above, too.

Five Questions to Ask Your Officiant

Your officiant's voice is the primary soundtrack of your ceremony. Who this person is might be a given (as it often is in many churches), or you might seek out a friend with a nice voice and public speaking experience.

Know who's who before you hire.

1. **Why do you officiate?** Look for someone who has an answer that resonates with you. This is someone you want to trust and see eye to eye with.

2. **Can you help us with the readings?** Can you provide us with options of traditional, nontraditional, secular, and religious readings we can choose from for our day? Can we provide our own options as well?

3. **How will we order the ceremony?** Some officiants have more flexible outlines than others. Yours can help familiarize you with the parts of a ceremony—opening prayer, remembrances, declaration of support, etc.—from which you can choose to include or omit.

4. **Will you record yourself reading through the ceremony?** Ask your officiant to send a video file or private YouTube link of her practicing your ceremony. You want to find out if she's mispronouncing your names well before the moment it matters.

5. **Will you be at the rehearsal?** The answer should be yes!

Choosing Your Stylist

The stylist is one vendor you can (and should) try out before the wedding day.

Look for someone with experience in not just hair and makeup, but *bridal* hair and makeup. You want someone well versed in pulling off multiple looks by the time the processional begins.

If you already have a stylist you trust, he is a good place to start. Be sure that whoever you consider isn't a one-trick pony. Ask him to demonstrate various styles so that you can decide what looks nicest on you and your bridesmaids.

For the trial run:

- Visualize what you want. Print pictures of styles you like and bring them with you.

- Be open to your stylist's ideas. Sometimes what you think you want isn't what you end up loving.

- Simulate your dress. Wear a shirt with a neckline and color similar to your gown's, so you can see how hairstyles work with it.

- Try the 'do with accessories. Bring the veil, tiara, or headband you plan to wear.

• **Take pictures.** Have someone photograph you from the front, both sides, and behind. You will be photographed more on your wedding day than probably any other day of your life, so you'll want to know—and like—what you look like from all angles.

Figuring Out the Flowers

Experienced florists are amazing resources. They deliver beauty despite only being given a budget and a loose vision. Here's what to keep in mind when you talk about blooms.

- **Seasonality.** April showers don't bring November flowers. You can order tulips during winter, but expect to be charged for the shipping from some place where the soil isn't frozen.

- **Delivery.** Will your florist drop off the flowers ahead of time, or will they be on-site to pin boutonnieres and assist with corsages?

- **Cost.** One of the biggest mistakes brides make is setting their sights on a flower without knowing its cost. So pick your top choice, but have a backup.

- **Bad weather.** Your florist will know if a particularly inclement season has adversely impacted the flowers you've ordered.

You can also attempt the floral situation yourself. Research what you want and where to get it.

The Bouquet

In much the same way that dresses flatter certain shapes and sizes, not every bouquet is built for every bride. Cascade bouquets—those that seem to spill over with flowers—can overwhelm a short frame, for example. When picking bouquets, consider weight (because you and your maids will hold them for prolonged periods), and how the color(s) look against the backdrop of the gowns. Texture (think berries or branches) adds nice dimension to the right combination.

No one said you have to use flowers at all. Nowadays, bouquets feature:

- Vegetables (google "kale bouquets"!)
- Buttons and brooches
- Clutches with decorative flowers
- Books
- And a lot more—be creative!

Here's an interactive bouquet idea: If you're looking to involve guests in the ceremony, collect flowers from them as you walk the aisle. Have someone at the ready to tie them all together.

Ceremony and Centerpiece Arrangements

Not sure where to begin? A few tips:

- Choose flowers associated with something special to you: a family member, a place, or a sorority, for example.

- Let your wedding date dictate your options. Nothing says fall like mums and pumpkins. Plus, in-season options cost less!

- Be cognizant of where the flowers will be. Avoid colors that clash with the venue.

- Done carrying the bouquets? Stick them in vases on your bar or tables.

- Outfit tables with potted herbs or plants that guests can take home as favors. Kill two birds with one . . . stem.

- Go *un*real. Think about handmade paper flowers or silk blooms, which are lovely and less agitating to anyone with allergies. But beware: nice-looking fake flowers can cost just as much as real ones. Of course, they won't wilt, so you can keep or peddle your petals afterward.

Arranging Transportation

Maybe you want to be photographed at two or three locations. Maybe you want a vehicle with enough room for a certain bride in a certain large, ivory dress to easily and elegantly exit. Or maybe you want a shuttle to escort your guests back to their hotel at the end of the night. Regardless, here's what to ask when hiring your wheels:

- Do you have proof of appropriate licensure? What level of insurance do you carry?

- May I see the actual vehicle?

- What's your minimum booking time?

- How many passengers does the vehicle accommodate comfortably?

- Does the vehicle's climate control work? Does it turn off when idling?

- Do you know the area where you'll drive us?

How to Select Your Attendants

Soon, it'll be *your* turn to pop the question. Choose your bridesmaids and groomsmen well. These are roles that require people's time, money, and dependability.

- Location. Know your wedding's size, location, and theme before you plan the bridal party. Large wedding parties can look out of place at quaint weddings.

- The right fit. Ask yourself: who knows us best, who's reliable and helpful, and who would truly appreciate standing beside us as we make this commitment?

- Less is more. Do you really need ten bridesmaids? Bear in mind: these are people you'll need to herd through the various parts of wedding planning and the wedding itself and for whom you'll buy gifts.

- No pressure. Don't be pressured to make someone a part of your bridal party. Not everyone needs to be in it to be included in the occasion. Ask someone special to deliver a reading or usher during the ceremony, give a toast at dinner, bring breakfast the morning of, or the like.

- Ask away. Brides today are asking their friends to do them the honor in any number of creative and moving ways. Consider incorporating your colors, your theme, or your favorite memories when you do it. Or tie a "love ya!" balloon to a small broom and dustpan set and see if your sister gets it. (Get it? Maid?)

- Be thankful. Show your gratitude often. Give cards. Bring snacks and bottled water for long bridesmaid dress shopping excursions.

- More help. Don't forgo help that's offered from others because you feel like you should lean on your bridal party only. You're planning the largest party you'll likely ever throw. Why would you turn down genuine offers of assistance?

How to Find the Dress

Your gown is the greatest reveal of the day. It is also one dress in an ever-churning sea of white, ivory, champagne, and you-name-the-color silhouettes. How does a bride choose?

1. **Research.** Identify dress styles you like, and figure out what sorts of accessories you want to incorporate into your look.

2. **Pick a place to shop.** Consider big-name retailers and boutique stores as well as trunk shows, where designers sell directly to brides. Sometimes, such shows offer killer deals. Don't rule out your local department store, too. When you choose your dress shop, search its website for gowns it sells. Jot down the names or numbers of dresses you'd like to try on.

3. **Pick a peanut gallery.** You might be pressured to involve people you don't truly want to involve in dress shopping. Some bridal shops limit the size of the group you can bring; blame the shop if you feel the need to defend a non-invitation. Bring those whose opinions you value, but listen most to your own. If you're worried about

members of your peanut gallery being uncomfortable criticizing something you're wearing, make them signs they can vote with silently even if they don't have something specific to say.

4. **Pack your camera.** Lighting and mirrors can deceive.

5. **Try on gowns,** and not just the ones you came specifically to see. Sometimes, a gown you never would have taken off the rack slips on you like a gorgeous glove. Ask the bridal shop consultant to select a few dresses. Odds are, she's dressed a bride whose figure is similar to yours.

6. **Manage your expectations.** The dress-shopping experience can be overhyped. Some women find their dress the very first time they exit the dressing room. Others try on 20-plus options. Some never cry happy tears.

7. **Take your figure into account:**

   • Stark white may be the convention but isn't always flattering for curvier figures and fairer complexions.

- Higher waistlines, such as empire waistlines, create the illusion of long legs. Ball gowns can overwhelm small figures.

- Capped sleeves help hide shoulders. Longer, looser sleeves cover up arms.

- A dark-colored sash or belt is one way to make your waistline look trimmer, and ruching helps hide midsection imperfections. A-line gowns help conceal curves below the waist.

- Diagonal lines create a slimming effect, but be careful: if they lean more horizontal, they can add bulk.

- Mermaid gowns create the hourglass effect for women who want to appear curvier. The name is quite fitting—mermaid gowns can be hard to walk in.

- A square neckline does its part to conceal a bustier chest. Straps support larger assets, too.

8. **Sit in the gowns you're considering.** You want something fairly comfortable. Be cognizant, too, that heavy beading at the top of a gown can hurt your underarms.

9. **Always order bigger than you need.** Taking in a gown is easier than expanding it.

10. **Alterations.** You didn't spend this much to have the dress not fit you superbly. You'll want it hemmed, cups added if you disdain strapless bras, and a bustle added so your train is out of the way for the party. Dare to request bigger changes, too: Have an expert create a sweetheart neckline. Transform Grandma's dress into your dress. Add straps and capped sleeves. Decrease or increase the volume of your skirt. Start fittings roughly six weeks out, and hire someone with bridal gown experience. Be sure to bring your shoes, undergarments, jewelry, and other accessories to your fittings.

Regarding Toasts

There are many moments that, when left to spontaneity, light up your wedding night. Toasts tend not to be one of them.

- Choose your speakers. Often, toasts are given by the best man, the father of the bride, and someone who says a prayer. But if you want your mother, maid of honor, and/or sister to speak, ask them to do you that honor.

- Keep it short. Tell your speakers to keep it short and sweet (1 to 2 minutes). Remember, the longer the speeches, the less time for mingling and festivities.

- Keep it nice. Choose people you can trust to recognize that there is a time and place for everything; you don't want to be embarrassed (intentionally or not) on your wedding day.

- Don't open the mic. When people aren't prepared, they may go on and on—worse yet, about topics you wish they wouldn't. Besides, you may suffer an awkward silence if no one pipes up to toast you.

- **Ward off rogue toasts.** Have your emcee intercept any unplanned speakers. Ask your master of ceremonies to watch for uncomfortable moments; your DJ or emcee can ensure a suddenly malfunctioning, conveniently muted microphone.

- **Schedule toasts early.** It should help avoid slurry speeches. Or request that anyone making a toast observe a pretoast drink limit.

- **Say a word yourselves.** It's meaningful for guests, some of whom may not spend much time with you newlyweds, to hear a welcome and thanks from you. This is the first time you address people as your newly married self. Have fun, and make it count.

**Detail
Stuff**

How to Handle Showers and Parties

Traditionally, the bridal shower and bachelorette party are not for you to plan. But they are thrown in your honor, so share your preferences if asked. And be gracious even if you aren't consulted.

Questions you may be asked by the bridesmaid, friend, or parent planning the event include:

- **Do you want a large crowd or a more intimate gathering?** Heads-up: you'll need to provide the names and addresses of the people you want invited.

- **What sort of shower would you like?** A shower can be anything from a formal party to a casual lunch.

- **What preferences do you have for the party?** Sultry stuff or elegant and low-key? Games or no games? A one-night get-together or a weekend excursion? Coed or just you and your girls?

- **When would you like the event to happen?** The night before your wedding may not be the best time for a wild bachelorette party.

- **Any special requests?** Parties don't have to involve embarrassing games. For example, your guests could shower you with their own family recipes (and an accompanying spice) to start your collection.

If you're being showered with gifts, enlist someone to keep a log of who gave you what while you open them. It will help you immensely when you write thank-you notes afterward. And hosting these parties can prove expensive and time-consuming, so save some special thanks for the planners.

Selecting the Gifts *You* Give

Without the support of parents, bridesmaids, and groomsmen, weddings would be a far more stressful beast, if you can imagine that. So we thank them all with gifts.

For Parents

- A photobook with images of the wedding (to be given afterward)

- A picture frame engraved with a message

- A gift card to their favorite restaurant

- A massage

- Something that reflects their interests (perhaps a monthly subscription that delivers a spice, hot sauce, wine, chocolate, etc.)

For Bridesmaids and Groomsmen

- T-shirts or sweatshirts sporting home team pride

- Tote bags filled with things for the big day (snacks, lip gloss, flip-flops, bobby pins, etc.)

- Jewelry

- Personalized beer mugs and a six-pack of their favorite beer (same concept can be adapted for wine connoisseurs)

- Items they can find only in your wedding city, such as locally made soap, jelly, or wine

- Haircuts and styling

- Slippers

- Sunglasses

- Personalized jerseys

Dressing Your Wedding Party

Bridesmaid dresses are cliché for a reason: even if your friends love their satin tea-length clover gowns while walking down the aisle, they may never wear them again. So try to remember these items when selecting your attendants' attire:

- **Match the tone.** Whether you choose tuxedos or khakis, elegant evening gowns or short party dresses, your bridal party's wear should make sense for your wedding's theme and feel.

- **Consider location.** Let the setting and time of year dictate what your bridesmaids wear. Faux fur shawls add an exquisite (and warm!) touch to wintery bridesmaid wear, whereas lightweight, flowing dresses and bare feet contribute naturally to the feel of a beachfront wedding. The same goes for the men: tuxedos are suave, but if you're getting married at a lodge with a taxidermied bear on the wall, the vest-and-slacks look makes a lot more sense.

- **Budget appropriately.** It's your wedding, but it's their money. Be sure to ask your bridal party (both bridesmaids and groomsmen) what they can afford, and then respect their budgets.

- **Talk accessories.** Choose shoes, hairstyles, and jewelry for your bridesmaids, or leave these decisions up to them. Just let them know which it is. And if you require a particular hairstyle on the day of your wedding, plan to pay for them to have it done.

- **Be creative.** Here are some lesser-used options for achieving the right look:

  - Pick a color, and have your bridesmaids choose dresses in a hue they prefer.

  - Go with little black dresses. Choose an accessory to tie the looks together.

  - Dress your maid or matron of honor in a slightly different color or style from other attendants so that everyone can easily see who your right-hand woman is.

  - Bow ties, suspenders, jackets on, jackets off, sunglasses, and ties: options abound for the men in your party, too, but set the tone first with the women's attire.

  - Dare to pick a print for bridesmaid dresses, bow ties, or socks.

- Pick an era, rather than a color or style, and take the bridesmaids and groomsmen to a vintage store to shop.

How to Accessorize Your Wedding Look

Now that you have the perfect gown, it's time to personalize. If you're feeling indecisive, ask advice from family, bridesmaids, and/or your tailor (after all, she's likely seen hundreds of bridal looks).

Hair

- Veil styles run the gamut, from birdcage to cathedral. Lengthy veils can be a nightmare for outdoor ceremonies.

- Headband or headpiece

- Hair clips and/or stylized bobby pins

- Tiara

Jewelry

- Earrings

- Bracelets

- Necklace

- Rings

- Anklet

Other Accessories

- Gloves

- Parasol

- Bridal mask

- Shawl or shrug

- Belt or sash

A Note about Shoes

Your wedding day isn't the day to start wearing heels if all you ever wear are flats. Your walk down the aisle will be one of the day's most-watched events; be comfortable, not pained or awkward. Take your wedding shoes to your fittings so your gown is hemmed properly to accommodate their height. And don't be afraid to make your shoes (or tights) a color pop.

Selecting Your Rings

This is it: the jewelry you two will wear every day, ever after. Choose wisely and well.

- **Talk it over.** Picking out rings for each other may seem romantic, but forever is a long time, and you want to be sure you both like the selections.

- **Timing is everything.** Give yourself plenty of time to shop around, purchase your rings, have them sized, and have them soldered and cleaned before your big day. If you're a stock size (in general, 10 for men, 7 for women), you won't need as much time for sizing.

- **Consider utility.** If you work with heavy machinery, a hard metal such as titanium may be a better bet than something softer (e.g., gold).

- **Go online.** Some shoppers vet only the retailers and wholesalers in their area, but rings can be purchased from websites such as Etsy, Amazon, and Overstock, too.

- **Go heirloom.** Some brides choose jewelry passed down from a previous generation.

- **Customize it.** Options for personalizing your rings include engravings, adding one or both of your birthstones, opting for a center stone that isn't a diamond, or designing your ring entirely. (This takes longer!)

- **Do your research.** Brush up on the 4 Cs (cut, carat, color, and clarity). Some people consider the supply chain, too. You may want to find out if your diamond was mined in a war zone, for example. Gold and tungsten are considered "conflict" minerals, too.

- **Prepare for the future.** If you have your heart set on eventually wearing a band on either side of your engagement ring, bear in mind that styles may be discontinued before a future anniversary. It may be best to take both bands home and stow one away for later.

Gift Registry Tips

What you ask to receive is a reflection of you and the life you hope to build with your future spouse. And filling out the registry can be a fun opportunity to imagine that life together! Your wish list will be unique to you, but this general advice will get you started:

- Keep it separate. Your wedding invitation is not the place to share registry specifics. Do it, instead, on a separate insert, with a shower invitation, on a wedding website, or through word of mouth.

- Add what you need. Traditionally, the registry is used for the things you need to set up your household. That could mean a crockpot, a set of knives, curtains and curtain rods, linens and towels, china, a mixer or other kitchen wizardry, or anything else you will use.

- Think outside the gift bag. If a list of new household items doesn't appeal to you, there are plenty of other options: an Amazon registry, a wedding vendor registry (to help fund some aspect of the wedding you want but perhaps can't afford), money or gift cards toward your honeymoon or a larger purchase (like furniture), donations to a charitable cause in your name, or no registry at all.

- **Track the gift cards.** If you do receive gift cards, make sure to follow up with the giver after you spend them and tell the person what their gift afforded you.

- **Register for a variety of price points.** Give your guests plenty of options so they can spend as much or as little as they want.

Invitations 101

The invitations are your guests' first taste of the wedding to come. The details you choose—the artwork, colors, calligraphy, and fonts—will set the stage.

Save-the-Date Cards

These identify to guests, before all of your wedding details are ironed out, the date you've chosen. Send them six to nine months before the wedding and even earlier if it's a destination wedding. Information to include:

- Your wedding date, including the day of the week, especially if you aren't marrying on a Saturday

- Where it will be, especially if you're asking people to travel

- A note that tells guests a formal invitation will follow

Invitations

Invites and enclosures, or the ancillary pieces of information you include, are what signal to guests what kind of ceremony and ensuing party you're hosting. Be sure to see a sample invitation before ordering dozens, even hundreds. Send them two or three months before the wedding. Information to include on the invitations, enclosures, and/or a wedding website (if you make one):

- Your full names

- Wedding date and time

- Addresses of the ceremony and reception venues and a map with landmark-specific directions. If a right turn is after a gas station, say so.

- A heads-up if the wedding is outside, so your guests can dress accordingly

- Another heads-up if it's an adults-only event

- A list of area restaurants and activities if you suspect people will stay in your wedding locale for longer than your big day. Visitors bureaus and elected officials' offices are great sources for local favorites.

- Hotel information if you've blocked hotel rooms (which you should do, and do early if the wedding is on a holiday weekend). Share the room rate and the date by which your guests must make reservations.

RSVP Cards

These are cards you provide (with self-addressed stamped envelopes) for guests to return, identifying how many will attend and meal choice, if you ask for it. If you worry that guests will bring people you didn't invite, type the names of the individuals who are actually welcome on the RSVP card.

These cards are ultimately for your use. Keep them plain and simple, or be creative if you plan to keep them as a souvenir. (RSVP Mad Libs, anyone?) Ask for them back a month before the wedding date. You'll want a little extra time to track down stragglers before providing head counts to vendors.

Other Paper

Here are some other ideas for your event's paper trail. Keep the fonts, colors, and design the same or similar to make your wedding look cohesive.

- A timeline of events

- A menu for each place setting

- A dessert guide or other informational guide to help your guests navigate the event

- Day-of thank-you notes for guests, ideally at each place setting

- Programs

Choosing Your Traditions

After the first kiss . . . comes a touchdown pass between a very committed NFL fan and his newly minted wife. That is to say, you can follow traditions, but you can also start your own. Think about including what's important to you or ask your mother or grandmother for family traditions to incorporate.

And of course you can choose from plenty of popular elements.

- Include photographs of loved ones.

- Plant a tree to symbolize the new branch you're beginning.

- Light a unity candle, pour sand into a glass container, or tie a knot (literally). All symbolize the joining of two into one.

- Include a blessing or ceremonial touch that reflects one or both of your heritages.

- Pass the rings among your guests. Each guest thinks a prayer or blessing upon your marriage while the rings are in their (brief) possession.

- Perform a first dance.

- Feed each other cake.

- Toss your bouquet and/or garter. The garter and bouquet tosses have been fairly ubiquitous. Some people love them, and some don't like the implication that their single guests should be so desperate to marry that they vie to snag them from the air.

How to Select Readings

Even if you grew up envisioning your wedding in intricate detail, you may have no idea what readings you'd like to hear during the ceremony.

- **Ask your officiant for help.** She may be able to provide you with the text of traditional and nontraditional and secular and religious options. Seeing a variety of choices will help you determine what you like and dislike.

- **Go online.** Wedding websites, search engines, and social media offer a ton of inspiration. Search for readings related to something important to you, be it trust, fidelity, friendship, or anything else.

- **Pick something that speaks to you.** If you both cry when you read it, put it on the short list. Consider having your officiant share a few sentences about why each reading speaks to you two.

- **Quote your favorites.** Have a favorite movie, book, play, poem, or song? Pick a quotation or excerpt from it.

- **Fit the scene.** Consider matching the feel of your readings to the feel of your ceremony venue. If you're getting married outside in a wooded area, for example, find a reading that uses trees or roots as a metaphor.

- **Get personal.** It may not be a reading per se, but a short selection about how the two of you tick, how you met, or how you got engaged can function in the same way.

How to Write Your Vows— Or Not

Wedding vows are the words that render silent any crowd. They are the true culmination of the time you've spent putting this day together.

Traditional Vows

Traditional vows are popular for a reason. It's pretty neat to know you're speaking the same words that have bound people together time and time again. And certainly you can make adjustments: If a word or phrase bothers you, remove it. (Looking at you, "obey.") If you want a little bit of personalization, add a sentence or two.

Writing Your Own

Thinking about penning your vows? They're arguably the most powerful words you'll ever utter (no pressure!). But don't feel like you have to write them yourself just because it's different. Write them because it feels more personal. Write them because it would make you happy. Write them because you are a writer, so self-authored vows are truest to you. Or write them because traditional vows just don't speak to you. Here are some tips.

- **Start early.** At the very least, start keeping notes about sweet moments, reasons why this is all worth it, and promises you want to make as soon as you can. Start a rough draft of your vows at least two months before the big day. Write, read it another day, edit, and rewrite as many times as it takes. Give yourself time to really refine what you're going to say.

- **Keep them balanced.** Agree to a general structure, tone, and length with your partner. You don't want to realize at the altar that your spouse-to-be is making you five promises, and you didn't speak one.

- **Take a positive tone.** Now is not the time to roast your spouse.

- **Make it personal.** Ideas include:

  - Fond memories. Keep them brief and accessible to everyone.

  - Specific promises.

  - Expressions of love and appreciation. It's okay to be raw; your guests will bring tissues.

- **Take a deep breath.** Baring your soul in front of a room full of people—and writing the words you'll use to do so—can be nerve-wracking. But so long as it's your truth, it's the day's truth. You'll be surrounded by people who love you, and they will hang on your words, not criticize them. So speak as slowly and loudly as you can, pause if you need to collect yourself, and, if all else fails, pretend you two are the only ones there.

Setting the Day-Of Timeline

A schedule of events is helpful for your vendors, your bridal party, your parents—and you. Establish one ahead of time and try to stick to it as closely as possible. Here's how.

- **Ask the experts.** This isn't your wedding vendors' first rodeo, so one surefire way to allot enough time for hair, photography, and the like is simply to ask these pros how long things will take.

- **Cushion your times.** Delays are inevitable.

- **Stay in one place.** As much as you can, anyway. Ask stylists to come to you at the venue or your hotel. It saves you the driving.

- **Shoot beforehand.** Although it breaks with tradition, slating some photos before the ceremony means fewer will need to be shot between the wedding and reception.

Remember to outline everything, including these easily overlooked details:

- Where your photographer should begin the day, and everywhere she should visit before the ceremony

- Time for corsage pinning

- What time you and your bridesmaids should arrive at the ceremony venue (you want to be hidden from view long before early birds begin to flock there!)

- The times at which toasts should be delivered and/or the order in which they should be given

How to Personalize Your Programs

They aren't mandatory, but guests appreciate programs because they tell them what to expect.

- **Start with a timeline.** Include ceremony events like the processional, readings, vows, ring exchange, pronunciation of marriage, and recessional. Don't hesitate to add the elements you've personalized, too. Maybe you will call out a "Gratitude" element when your officiant thanks guests for spending the day with you, an "Introductions" element when she will identify your parents and the important role they've played in your lives, or even "The Kiss."

- **Include the reception.** Often the program covers just the ceremony, but you could conclude with a reception timeline. Guests are comfortable when they know what's going on. A schedule of events taking place after the ceremony could tell them not only how long they have before the reception starts, but when your grand entrance, dinner, dessert, and dancing will begin.

- **Introduce the cast.** Programs often identify your parents by name. You can also use them to introduce your bridal party—by name, description, caricature, or whatever else makes sense.

- **Get creative.** Try handheld fans for warm weddings, front-page newspapers for journalists, playbills for theater-themed weddings, messages in bottles for nautical-themed weddings, or something different that best fits your event.

- **Keep in theme.** The more cohesive your paper materials, the more branded and elevated your event. Wherever possible, extend the fonts, colors, fabrics, and motifs of your invitations and/or decorations to your programs.

How to Pick Favors

Favors are a key way a bride and groom show gratitude to those who spend the day celebrating with them. The problem with simply giving something impersonal and of limited use is that you'll likely end up with dozens of them. Many a caterer will tell you that guests often leave favors behind. If you suspect that might happen, order fewer than you need and set up a favor table rather than placing one at each setting. That way, guests who want them can take them, and those who don't won't leave you cradling dozens of personalized shot glasses at the end of the night. Here are more ways brides are approaching the favor dilemna.

- **Something practical.** Options include beer koozies, heart-shaped measuring spoons, planters of herbs such as basil or thyme, and cookie cutters, to name a few.

- **Something local.** It's a nice touch—and another opportunity to personalize your event—to give your guests something made in town. Think about wine, honey, or soap, for example.

- **Something homemade.** Is there something *you* can make and give as a token of your appreciation? Perhaps a family recipe, accompanied by its secret ingredient, or handmade bird feeders? The possibilities abound, but, as with anything do-it-yourself, start earlier than you think you need to. You have enough to do as the wedding nears without getting buried in birdfeed.

- **Something charitable.** Forgoing favors is increasingly popular. Many brides opt to donate to a charity on behalf of their guests instead.

- **Something memorable.** Give your guests something with which to remember the night. Hire a photo booth or bring in an artist to draw their caricatures, for example.

Picking a Guestbook

Options abound for how guests can leave you well-wishes. Popular choices include:

- Album.

- Scrapbook. Have your guests sign pieces of paper. Assemble a scrapbook later.

- Quilt. Provide fabric pens and fabric for your guests to sign. Quilt them together later.

- Photo. Have guests sign a matte.

- Book of questions. Write questions on the pages of a blank book for guests to answer. Make them relationship themed, like "What's the key to a successful marriage?"

- Suggestion boxes. Ask guests to drop marriage advice into boxes labeled "first anniversary," "first married fight," "first baby," or other landmarks.

Eight Steps to Seating Everyone

Like everything else, seating takes some organization. That's not to say it has to be complicated. Here's how to put everyone in the proper place.

1. **Source the furniture.** Options abound if you've chosen a venue for which chairs and tables are yours to find. Do you want long rectangular tables or rounds? Vintage pieces or modern?

2. **Handle the details.** A traditional venue will supply chairs and tables. But even then, you may have choices: Do you rent chair covers and/or chair sashes? Do you commission other furniture that fits your theme?

3. **Consider your seating.** Popular options include a traditional head table seating your entire bridal party and a sweetheart table seating just the two of you.

4. **Assign seating.** If you assign guests to tables, it will be one of the last things you do, because you will need their RSVPs first. Draw a floor plan of your venue on poster board and stick

guests' names to it with post-it notes. If you need to move someone to another table, pull off the post-it and relocate his name. Begin by seating those to whom you're closest . . . closest to you. Seat anyone you know may not get along away from one another. And fill in the seating chart from there.

5. **Be flexible.** There's no reason you can't assign some people so they're where you want them and leave others to sit where they please.

6. **Number the tables.**

7. **Plan for kids.** Consider designating a kids' corner and providing crayons.

8. **Arrange for a vendors' table.**

How to Make Your Guests Comfortable

They call it your day, but keeping your guests happy and comfortable means that they'll stay longer and you'll all have more fun.

Weather

- You can't control the rain clouds gathering above your gazebo, but planning ahead can prevent—or at least mitigate—discomfort.

- Tell guests in your invitations if the ceremony will be outside. That warns them to dress appropriately and bring sunblock.

- Expect it to be hot? Consider stylized fans, water bottles, and sunglasses. Also, ask your venue staff when they will turn on the A/C and how long it takes to cool the space.

- Fear rain? Outfit your guests with dated umbrella favors or ponchos.

- Will it be chilly? Line up patio heaters.

Timing and Location

- Provide a timeline. It affords your guests a glimpse of what's next and tells them where they need to be and when.

- If you can avoid doing so, don't schedule three hours of waiting between your ceremony and reception. Limit the interim to one hour, and don't leave your guests idle: serve appetizers (even a simple cheese platter will do), have your venue pour some drinks, and entertain.

- Logistically speaking, hosting the ceremony and reception at the same locale is convenient, especially for out-of-town guests.

- Have a bag, complete with a map and a list of things to do and eat in the area, placed in guests' hotel rooms. Define (to a tee, using crystal-clear landmarks) where the ceremony and festivities will go down.

Little Mouths

- If you prefer not to have children at the reception, it can be easier on parents if you provide/identify an on-site babysitting service.

- Engage your youngest guests with kids' activity packs.

On Their Seat, and Their Feet

- Worried about the simple folding chairs? Rent chair cushions.

- If your friends love to dance, consider buying a box (or more) of dollar-store flip-flops.

How to Obtain a Marriage License

Getting a marriage license is not something to leave to the last minute. Without it, you're not officially wed. Call your county court and ask:

- Do I need to get my marriage license in the county where I'm getting married or the county in which I live?

- How much does a marriage license cost?

- What forms of payment do you accept? What forms of identification do we need?

- How soon before our wedding day must we have the license, and how soon after it's in hand must we marry?

- When does our marriage become official (if that's important to you)? That is, if the officiant signs it before the ceremony, are we already married when we exchange vows?

Wedding
(and Beyond)
Stuff

Nurturing Your Relationship

As wedding planning starts to pick up steam, one thing that may start to fall to the bottom of your to-do list is, ironically, your relationship with your spouse-to-be. Here's how to keep your bond strong.

Share the Planning–or Don't

Your partner may be as invested in brainstorming floral arrangements and obsessing over hors d'oeuvres as you are. Congratulations! Having a significant other who's interested in the planning process not only means you have someone with whom to share responsibilities, it can also deepen the importance of the wedding itself because it is the result of both your energies and efforts. If this sounds like your partner, take advantage of the extra help and divvy up responsibilities or schedule regular meeting times for you to put your heads together and tag-team the big day.

However, your future spouse may be the sort whose eyes may glaze over every time you open your mouth because you're talking nonstop about some wedding detail or another. Don't sweat it if your partner prefers to be as far away from all planning responsibilities as possible. When both your heads are cool, discuss that you need help with some tasks and together find a few that you can hand off—such as scheduling day-of transportation if he's a logistics whiz or mulling over menu options if he's a foodie.

Make Time for Each Other

Regardless of how much one or both of you is loving (or hating) the planning process, it's important for the two of you to enjoy time with each other—because your relationship is the whole point of this wedding, after all. Schedule a date night or weekend trip when wedding talk is fully off limits, and commit to really being present one another. Even if your schedules allow for only a night off from planning, this time together will reinforce your connection and remind you that all the stress is worth it.

Talk It Out

Premarital counseling may sound scary if you've never sought out a therapist before, or you might think it's only for people who are experiencing difficulties. In fact, meeting with a professional trained to work with couples can help you and your partner maintain a healthy relationship during the planning process and start to envision your married life before it starts, by addressing topics like shared finances, whether you want children (and when), communication styles, and what you do and don't expect of each other after you're married. The American Association for Marriage and Family Therapy offers a therapist locator tool on its website (aamft.org).

Rehearsal Essentials

As with any production involving multiple people, a rehearsal of your wedding is clutch. Here's a handy checklist to peruse a day or two before the big day:

Rehearse the Ceremony

☐ Try to practice in the same space you'll be marrying in. Invite your bridal party and parents, other close family if you'd like, and anyone you've asked to do a reading.

☐ Cover the processional and recessional.

☐ Decide where each groomsman and bridesmaid should stand.

☐ Practice the exchange, if you've planned one, between your parent and the officiant.

☐ Have your officiant guide you through an outline of the ceremony (without actually pronouncing you married!).

☐ Have anyone who's doing a reading practice it.

Throw a Rehearsal Dinner

☐ Invite everyone who attended the rehearsal, but don't feel obligated to limit the guest list to them. Other family members, out-of-town guests, and the dates of members of your bridal party are common add-ons. When it comes to destination weddings, many brides extend a dinner invite to all guests, because most will be in town when it takes place.

☐ Throw a party! Whether it's a formal dinner or burgers and baked beans at a park pavilion, relax and enjoy yourselves with your closest supporters.

☐ Have your gifts ready. Rehearsal dinners are traditionally when you give thank-you gifts to your parents and bridal party.

Tipping Your Vendors

You depend on them to run things smoothly. To put out fires. To have uncomfortable conversations on your behalf. ("I'm sorry, we truly don't have that song in our library.") So when vendors meet—and certainly if they exceed—your expectations, tip them.

It's customary to tip the bartender, catering staff, hair and makeup stylists, your nondenominational officiant or the house of worship, people delivering items to the venue, wedding planners, and the limo driver. Be sure to double-check what you've paid already; some contracts include gratuity.

There are other vendors for whom tips are less expected—especially business owners—but nonetheless appreciated: DJs, photographers, and videographers.

Have someone you trust dole out the checks. As a rule of thumb, a 15 to 20 percent tip is appropriate. That said, when a vendor really comes through (redoing a hairstyle last-minute, flawlessly executing plan B when your outdoor ceremony gets rained out, etc.), no one will question your additional generosity.

Professional photographs showcasing vendors' work are nice tokens of appreciation, too. A gorgeous shot of your gown or the crowded dance floor could help them secure future business.

Send a thank-you card or e-mail after the event. And, for those vendors who really knocked it out of the park, give the tips that pay the greatest dividends: raving reviews, social media shout-outs, and blogger love.

How to Postpone or Cancel

Planning a wedding can become an uncomfortable juggling act of other people's feelings. It can stress out even the most compatible couples.

If you and your spouse-to-be are fighting more, here's what to do.

- Step back. Evaluate your motives. Are you arguing because the boutonnieres will have lasting importance, or are there deeper issues? If you suspect your tensions are rooted in the stress of wedding planning, remember: it is *one* day.

- Deal with parents. If your issues involve parents (very common during wedding planning), don't be afraid to tell them you are grateful for their support but they need to allow you and your spouse-to-be to create a wedding that reflects *you*.

- Think big picture. What truly matters is that, by the end of it all, you two will be happy and married.

Making the Call

If a voice in your head still says something isn't right, it may be best to postpone or cancel. Kathy Dawson, an Ohio-based relationship coach, says, "What is your motive for not cancelling? If the answer is, 'I don't want to cancel because people are expecting it,' that is the worst reason to get married." Don't let what others will think or the money already spent paralyze you. "Seriously, in the big picture, it's money. You'll make more. This is your life you're talking about."

Consider seeing a counselor or a relationship coach like Kathy, who in her twenties married although it didn't feel right. She has since divorced, remarried, and coached couples for more than twenty years through her practice, Kathy the Coach.

Spreading the Word

You aren't the first bride to postpone or cancel a wedding (and you won't be the last). Making this decision is a difficult move, but your guests will respect it. A few tips:

- **Tell those closest to you.** They should find out first, and face-to-face if possible. Develop an elevator speech, don't be too specific if you two are trying to work things out, and repeat your vague statement if people ask you to say more. If you stick to your boundaries, they'll stop asking.

- **Tell everyone else.** Handle your lists of invitees together, or divide it up and inform your section in your own way. Sending snail mail announcements is one way to formally and maturely inform would-be guests.

- **Ask for space.** If you're postponing, ask people to respect your privacy. Assure them that you'll let them know if and when the wedding is back on the calendar.

Coping

The end of a relationship is a raw, confusing time. Take care of yourself. Work out. Take a trip, or have close friends visit. Cry. Write down your feelings. See a professional. Grieve. Dig deep to gauge whether you're mourning the future you envisioned or the person from whom you've parted. Cry some more. And when you feel like it, smile again.

Handling Delicate Situations

This is likely the largest party you'll ever throw, and that means loads of food, drinks, and personalities in one room. Remember, you cannot control people. But you *can* plan for hiccups, tensions, and delicate situations. Here's how.

Planning Issues

- **Delegate.** If some people seem determined to make your event *their* event, delegate tasks judiciously. Having something to do will make them feel involved without forcing you to agree to details you don't want.

- **Stick to your guns.** If someone asks why you didn't invite them and you don't want to give your reason, blame the venue's size and fire code, which restricts a space's capacity.

- **Involve the mother of your spouse-to-be**, if possible. She might be eager to help but hesitant to ask, and she will have lots of insight into your soon-to-be family, too.

Family Friction

- **Ask.** Expecting familial tension? Ask your loved ones what would make them feel comfortable during potentially awkward or difficult moments such as family portraits and reception introductions.

- **Divide up the planning.** If you're encountering a tug-of-war between families or divorced parents over certain wedding details, silo the input you'll accept from each of them, arbitrarily or based on what they're paying for.

- **Communicate with your vendors.** Consider formally seating all mother figures and providing boutonnieres and corsages for all parents and stepparents to avoid hurt feelings. If there are people who should be kept separate at all costs, identify them to your photographer ahead of time.

- **Deal with divorced parents.** Worried that one parent will be upset seeing a moment between you and the other parent, such as when your mom witnesses the father-daughter dance? Ask someone, preferably a vendor with some legitimate reason, to distract Mom or Dad when that moment is scheduled.

- **Repurpose traditions.** Dad or Mom not in the picture? Invent your own traditions to involve those who *are* present. There's no reason it can't be a mother-daughter dance!

- **Include your stepparents.** If both your parent and stepparent play active roles in your life, you can gracefully include them both in your big reveal in plenty of ways. Ask them to walk you down the aisle jointly, for example, or have one escort you part of the way and the other the rest of the way.

- **Take the pressure off.** If involving or excluding certain family members in announcements during the reception makes you uncomfortable, consider announcing only the bridal party.

Drinks and Drama

- **Conspire with the bartender.** Know someone who tends to get rowdy—or, worse yet, angry—when they drink a lot? Give your bartender a heads-up ahead of time. She probably has plenty of experience dealing with similar situations and will know what to do.

- **Lean on the wedding planner.** Want something said if a problem arises? A wedding planner can put his foot down and quell drama without being perceived as taking sides. So, too, could the best man.

Difficult Convos Cheat Sheet

Situation: Your bestie complains about money every time you mention that she still hasn't bought her bridesmaid dress.

What to say: "Is being in my wedding costing you too much? Let's find another way you can be involved."

Situation: Your parents are dictating the guest list because, as they've reminded you time and again, they are paying for the wedding.

What to say: "We're so thankful that you're helping us out financially with the wedding. Can we revise the budget together so we can invite a few more of our friends?"

Situation: Aunt Betty is *dying* to make your wedding cake, but you want to hire a professional.

What to say: "We've already found a baker we love, and we want you to be able to fully enjoy our celebration!"

Situation: A family friend gifted you a vase that wasn't on your registry and is definitely not your personal style.

What to say: Nothing. Return it if you can, donate it if you can't, and either way send a thank-you note.

Taking a Honeymoon

Planning a whole trip can feel more like punishment than fun when you're already planning a wedding. But vacationing is an opportunity to decompress, take lots of pictures of the first days of your married life, and celebrate together. Life can get busy fast, so enjoy this time when your family consists of just the two of you. Here are some things to think about as you begin planning.

- **Travel agent?** Especially if your heart is set on an international or all-inclusive destination, working with a travel agent has its benefits.Many agents have visited the very places you're considering, and they'll know the reputations of locales and resorts and quite a bit about travel costs.

- **Undecided on a destination?** Look for a place known for what the two of you love to do. A visitors bureau website will reveal whether a city is well suited for history buffs, seafood lovers, or those who've perfected their poker faces. Or think about places you've both always wanted to see.

- **Think locally.** Honeymooning closer to home has its benefits, too. Planning and traveling are easier, the trip is gentler on your budget, and the destination can become the spot where you celebrate anniversaries.

- **Budget well.** The spreadsheets don't disappear after the wedding is planned. Calculate how much you can afford, and add up how much you anticipate spending. Don't forget travel costs (both to and around your destination), hotels, three meals a day, activities and events, souvenirs, and a little extra for unexpected expenses. Keep track of exchange rates if traveling internationally.

- **Time it right.** Don't feel obligated to rush off to the airport the morning after. The wedding day is long, and taking time to recover and rest is a good idea.

- **Mini-moon.** Consider, too, the option of delaying the big excursion but celebrating right away with a more local "mini-moon" in the meantime.

- **Keep your name.** Speaking of airports, the name on your flight needs to match the name on your ID. Resist the urge to book in your soon-to-be name if you won't have legally changed it yet.

- **Share the news.** Tell people it's your honeymoon! Whether you're making reservations somewhere or simply chatting, feel free to share. You'll be showered with congratulations, and some venues will kick in an upgrade, surprise, or special deal for the occasion.

- Register for it. Consider setting up a honeymoon registry online. Include a link to it with your other registry information.

- Dress for the weather. Find out what the weather tends to be where and when you plan to travel. For example, you may want to avoid the Caribbean during hurricane season (or at least buy travel insurance).

- Relax. Once you get there, don't overschedule yourselves if you don't want to. Consider having a day when you two don't move an inch. Book on-site massages. Order takeout or indulge with a personal chef. Enjoy whatever view you have.

- Get rewarded. Some people like to open a rewards credit card and use it to pay for big wedding expenses, earning points toward their travel. Be aware of any annual fees, however, and don't be reckless. No one wants to spend their first years of marriage drowning in debt created by a single day.

How to Change Your Name

When it comes to a surname switch, it truly is to each her own. You might choose to:

- Keep your maiden name, perhaps because it connects you to your family or because it's a strong part of your identity.

- Take your partner's last name, perhaps because you like the tradition, because doing so cements the formation of your new family, because you prefer your partner's name, or even because your maiden name is mercilessly mispronounced!

- Make your maiden your middle name, and take your partner's last name.

- Take a new last name. It *can* be done!

- Hyphenate, with or without an actual hyphen. Be careful and specific when you're introducing yourself. Two last names are often mixed up, used interchangeably, hyphenated or unhyphenated, and/or combined on airline tickets and by IT departments.

- Go with some combination of the above, for different purposes. For example, you might take your partner's name legally but keep or hyphenate your maiden name in professional contexts.

If you do decide to change your name, get certified marriage licenses and start with the social security office and then the driver's license bureau. Other places to make the change are credit cards, bank accounts, insurance policies, car registration and property titles, and employee records.

The Checklist

You may be marrying in two years or two months, so this checklist is vaguely timed. That said, set target dates for each of your goals. Doing so can be a great help.

Remember: Every bride's priorities are different. Not every item on this checklist may apply to you. And if a high priority of yours appears below a lower one on this checklist, tackle what's most important to you first. Work ahead, book vendors early, start DIY projects before you think you have to, and ask your vendors if you're not sure when you should take care of something. They will know.

Right Away

☐ Insure your ring. (See page 18.)

☐ Compile a rough guest list. (See page 23.)

☐ Create a wedding e-mail account. When wedding-related promo e-mails continue after you're married—and they will—you'll be blissfully unaware.

☐ Attend a bridal show or two.

☐ Picture the kind of wedding you two want. (See page 21.)

☐ Look for venues that can accommodate your vision and the number of guests you want to invite. (See pages 32 and 35.)

☐ Research the costs of at least three vendors in each category (florist, caterer, photographer, etc.). Based on the prices in your market, align your expectations and set a budget. (See page 25.)

☐ Book a venue (for both the ceremony and the reception). Now you can officially book other vendors because you know your date. (See page 29.)

☐ Start a fitness regimen. Walk an hour a day, commit to the gym more days in a week than not, or even hire a trainer. You want to look good for your big day, sure, but working out is also a great stress reliever, and planning a wedding can be stressful. When you feel healthier, you look it.

Early Choices

☐ Hire a wedding planner. (See page 44.)

☐ Hire the vendor you adore the most. Chances are good that others adore them, too, and you don't want them to be already booked.

☐ Hire a photographer. (See page 40.) Most photographers include engagement photography in their wedding packages. Have yours taken early if you want to use them on save-the-date cards.

☐ Hire a videographer. (See page 43.)

☐ Choose your bridal party. (See page 66.)

Stay Ahead of the Game

☐ Shop for your gown. Buy it. (See page 68.)

☐ Arrange the music. (See page 54.) Don't wait until the eleventh hour to choose songs for your special dances and must-play and do-not-play lists.

☐ Arrange for a tasting with a caterer.

☐ Hire a caterer. (See page 45.)

☐ If your vision entails handmade anything, get started months before you think you have to. Stick to a schedule of working on crafty details once a week or once a month.

☐ Hire an officiant. (See page 58.) Decide what time your ceremony will begin.

☐ Send save-the-date cards. (See page 89.) Do it extra early if you're planning a destination wedding or for a holiday weekend.

☐ Select your partner's wedding look.

About Halfway There

☐ Choose what the bridal party will wear. (See page 80.)

☐ Taste-test desserts. Hire a baker. (See page 51.)

☐ Hire your style team. (See page 60.)

☐ Hire a florist. (See page 62.)

☐ Research hotels in your wedding city. Pick one or two to recommend to guests and block rooms to secure a discounted rate.

☐ Create invitations, or hire a designer to do them for you. (See page 89.)

☐ Purchase your wedding bands. (See page 85.)

☐ Find a tailor and schedule alterations to your gown. Usually, you'll have three fittings. By the first fitting, know how high a heel you will wear. For the final fitting, bring every accessory and see how it all comes together.

☐ Stay ahead of any DIY projects. (Seriously.)

☐ Have one or two hair and makeup trials.

☐ Choose a honeymoon destination and book flights, if need be. (See page 129.)

☐ Order the gifts you'll give to your parents and bridal party. (See page 78.)

☐ Select your bridal accessories. (See page 83.)

Clock's Tickin'

☐ Decide on readings and other ceremony details, and begin writing your vows, if you are. (See pages 94 and 96.)

☐ Hire a driver. (See page 65.)

☐ Set up one or two gift registries. (See page 87.)

☐ Finalize guest list. Send invites. (See page 89.)

☐ Enjoy any bridal shower or bachelorette parties thrown for you. Send thank-you notes. (See page 76.)

☐ Create a detailed timeline for the big day; share it with your vendors. (See page 99.)

☐ Be sure to keep gown alterations on schedule.

☐ Decide on a site for your rehearsal and dinner. Send invitations. (See pages 117 and 89.)

☐ Start assigning seating. (See page 106.)

☐ Finish everything you plan to DIY. Designate who will tear down the reception hall at the end of the night.

☐ Plan for any other details you want to include, such as programs (see page 101), favors (see page 103), or a guestbook (see page 105).

Last Weeks

☐ Share guest count with vendors, including the caterer, wedding planner, and bartender.

☐ Give your DJ your lists of must-plays and do-not-plays.

☐ Provide a finalized wedding day timeline to parents, vendors, and the bridal party.

☐ Send locations and a map to your driver.

☐ Share must-shoot lists with your photographer and videographer.

☐ Pick up your altered gown.

☐ Get your marriage license. (See page 111.)

☐ Finish writing your vows. Read them aloud.

☐ Pack for your honeymoon.

☐ Get a manicure and pedicure—or massage if you're feeling the pressure!

☐ Go on a final, premarriage date with your partner.

☐ Rehearse!

☐ Give your wedding planner or a trusted friend envelopes of checks to distribute to vendors.

Day Of and Beyond

☐ Eat breakfast.

☐ Get ready, and resolve: no matter what happens today, I'm smiling, because we're getting married.

☐ Do the deed. Many congrats!

☐ Go on your honeymoon.

☐ Send thank-you notes.

Acknowledgments

I only planned one wedding, but I offer the wisdom of many. Thank you to every bride, groom, wedding guest, vendor, and parent who selflessly shared successes, regrets, lessons learned, and more via Facebook and my blog. You know who you are.

Morgan Mason, I remain humbled by your introduction. Thank you, Tiffany Hill, for not only editing me, but for guiding me through the unfamiliar process. And thank you, Quirk Books, for the opportunity. It's been a true treat and a welcome challenge.

Finally, thank you, Steven, for making me your happy bride and happier wife, thank you to my family and friends for standing (and crafting) with me through the chaos, and thank you to the vendors who made our day perfectly us.